# Happiness FM

## Mary Dickins

## Burning Eye

BurningEyeBooks
Never Knowingly
Mainstream

Supported using public funding by
ARTS COUNCIL
ENGLAND

LOTTERY FUNDED

This edition published by Burning Eye Books 2020

www.burningeye.co.uk
@burningeyebooks

Burning Eye Books
15 West Hill, Portishead, BS20 6LG

ISBN 978-1-91157083-7

# Happiness FM

# CONTENTS

# HOW TO ADMINISTER A POEM
## IN AN EMERGENCY

For those in cardiac arrest
perhaps a mild pantoum is best.
If they need assistance quick,
a haiku sometimes does the trick.
If the patient won't come round,
revive them with some Ezra Pound.
If you cannot stop the bleed,
Bukowski may be what they need.
Dorothy Parker is a must
for those bewildered and concussed.
A couplet or profound quatrain
can calm the fear and ease the pain.
Make wisdom, pathos, cheer and wit
a part of every first-aid kit.

So,

if adrift without an anchor,
try an intravenous tanka.
If life itself is living hell,
locate a soothing villanelle.
And, for those who've lost all hope,
a little bit of Wendy Cope?
Use with care and, in addition,
adopt the recovery position.

# WITH THE BABUSHKAS ON THE BEACH

Behold.
The babushkas on the beach,
bare billowing bellies
like basking belugas
in bitty bikinis.

Blowsy, brash babushkas
boast brimful brassieres
abreast broad backs.

Bellowing bossy blessings.
Beguiling this bulging, bashful Brit.

Bravo,
beautiful brazen babushkas.

Bye-bye, brassy, bountiful,
bonkers babushkas.

# HAPPINESS FM

happiness is a radio station
you chance upon
that plays music
so sublime
you are immediately transported

next day you try to find it
but no matter
how long you scan the airwaves
it's drowned by crackling interference
sometimes
you hear snatches in the background
so you try again
and again
and again
and again
until you realise
that only fate decides the frequency
of Happiness FM

and some people have better reception
than others

# HOW TO DO YOUR BUCKET LIST
##    ON THE CHEAP

No savings? No trust fund? No final salary pension?
Don't be despondent; just deploy your powers of invention.
First find a clip of a flash mob choir and sing along to the *Messiah*.
Take an online tutorial daily. Learn a few chords on the ukulele.
Spanish and German, a smattering of these, and some
conversational Japanese.
Don't get ideas above your station. Content yourself with
simulation.


So tune in to Google Earth. Go to Delhi, then to Perth,
Phuket, Tromsø, Budapest, New Orleans and Marrakesh.
For each place try a national dish: thali, noodles, pickled fish,
fiery goulash, lamb tagine. Consume by the glow of your laptop
screen.
Find a nice boutique hotel, take a virtual tour and, hell,
wear shades, sombrero or sun visor. Leave complaints on
TripAdvisor.
Wear bobble hat and salopettes to watch skiing on the internet.
Send a tweet to the Dalai Lama, Yoko Ono and Obama.
Similarly Johnny Depp and anyone else you wish you'd met.
Lighten up. Don't feel a fool with your plastic dolphin at the local
pool.
Go on! Scamper naked in the dew. Get that ill-advised tattoo.


Some strategies must be employed to plug this existential void,
but if you find yourself depressed, egocentric, self-obsessed…
if you suspect that it's a sham, or a convoluted marketing scam –
if you find it hard to coexist with all the thrills you think you'll
miss,
that you might not drive a racing car or party at the Mardi Gras,
swim in the Sargasso Sea or get to know a chimpanzee,
hike the Appalachian Trail or help to save the humpback whale,
play the tuba in a band or visit mosques in Samarkand –
accept that it's beyond your reach to ride the surf at Bondi Beach,

to climb that distant mountain peak or teach a mynah bird to speak.
So stop this morbid quest. Desist!
And please destroy this bucket list.

# ACCESS DENIED

Your password has not been recognised. Access was denied.
We requested information, but you have not complied.
You can go on to our help page, but the questions won't apply.
According to our systems, your existence is a lie.

Your details have not been verified. Authentication failed.
You cannot access this account. Your plans have been derailed.
We admire your persistence and your rudimentary skill,
but you might be better suited to some parchment and a quill.

This message is auto-generated; please do not reply.
If you really *must* continue, click this button and retry.

# LOVE ON THE INTERNET

Our love is too vast for an email.
It can't be condensed to a tweet.
We Snapchat and Skype, but it's merely a hype
compared to the thrill when we meet.

It can't be configured in pixels,
reminders of places we've been.
It can't be summed up in a soundbite
displayed on an LCD screen.

Our love is much more than mere data.
Too complex. Too messy. Too fraught.
It can't be backed up on a server
or plugged in a USB port.

We can't close the distance between us.
There are too many miles to transcend.
These digital fragments are all that we have
and all we can do is click *send*.

# HONEST RETURNS

I am returning this item because…
*(Please select from the menu below.)*

- I am much fatter than I think I am.

- I was drunk when I ordered it.

- I was stoned when I ordered it.

- I only needed it for a party.

- I am not clever enough to assemble the flat pack.

- I misunderstood the dimensions.
  *(This baking tray is only big enough for one potato.)*

- I misunderstood the dimensions.
  *(My garden is too small for a 30-foot obelisk.)*

- It fails to fill the aching void inside me.

- I am renouncing the destructive and unsustainable trappings of western capitalism and going off-grid to live in a yurt.

- I did not mean to order a pack of two hundred.

- I realise I have absolutely no money left in my account.

# IT'S ALL GONE PICASSO

*If Picasso shared a house with other artists.*

Gilbert and George are in their rooms inspecting bits of poop
and that bloody Andy Warhol has taken all the soup.
The place is like a pigsty. Tracey Emin's gone to bed.
Van Gogh's experimenting with self-harming in the shed.
Damien's breeding butterflies. Dali's melted the clocks.
Gauguin and Toulouse-Lautrec have gone and got the pox.
Matisse has all the scissors. Can he really need them all?
Degas has ballerinas pirouetting in the hall.
Turner's gone all sulky. Holman Hunt just rants.
Dante Gabriel Rossetti needs to keep it in his pants.
Pissarro hates Pollock. Rembrandt can't abide Vermeer.
Banksy just pops in and out and only shows his rear.
Of course we all love Frida. I myself have tried,
but that hothead Leonardo had to take the fight outside.
This place is worse than Guernica, as I for one should know.
I'm off to found the Cubist movement. Adios.
Pablo

# DEAR PROFESSOR BRIAN COX

Dear Professor Brian Cox, we love to watch you on the box.
The wife and I have to confess it's not just the science about
which we obsess.
That time when you explained the quark, you ignited a certain
spark.
Soon we were having thoughts obscene whilst you described
the selfish gene.

We feel it timely to profess we'd love to meet you in the flesh!
Please forgive us if we say we'd like to share some DNA.
We'll explore this urge like an electronic surge; our
entanglement will be quantum.
The wife assures her celestial orbs can be yours whenever you
want 'em.

So, Brian, think on; if you can, come along to our Big Bang.
With sufficient frantic motion we might find our own Higgs
boson.
If our lust should make you weary, we could just discuss string
theory.

Now, please, Brian, don't be vexed. It isn't just about the sex.
We view your mind with great respect.

We wondered at the solar storms and the sludge where life
first formed.
We listened rapt as, with aplomb, you explained the atom
bomb.
You made clear to the entire nation the principle of gravitation,
the source of the rift in the continental drift, why planets circle
the sun,
how oceans formed, how life began and the laws of cell
mutation.

Brian, we will always dote on that breathless way you explain
the proton.

Even if it's not to be, we can watch your DVD.
You're on the television so much we don't really have to touch.
We can contemplate Uranus. Hypothesise about black holes.
Explore that darker energy. Flit with you from pole to pole.
We'd have loved to see you quite content between our
hypothermal vents,
but if you say no it could be worse.
There's always a parallel universe.

# ON SITTING NEXT TO JOHN COOPER CLARKE ON A TRAIN

Evidently it's Cooper Clarke. I'd know him even in the dark,
but to say, *Hi, John,* seems too familiar.
A wink would just be weird.
A nod? A continental kiss? I doubt that he would welcome this.
He might be sick of sycophantic puppets.
He might think, *Go away, you muppet.*
*And please don't show me that crumpled verse*
*that you've probably got tucked away in your purse.*
Even if I don't pose an immediate danger,
to him I am just a total stranger.
So I say nothing.
But it's hard.
Because at times when life has been truly shit,
I've reached for his volumes of Salford grit.
So I want to say,

*You're the punk pied piper.*
*You're a syllable sniper.*
*You're a slick soothsayer.*
*You're a jargon slayer.*
*You're a peptic collector of sceptic wit.*
*A louche lounge lizard with a lot of lip.*
*You're a scene shapeshifter with an urban vista.*
*A true-grit, dropkick, comeback mister.*
*You're a verbal viper – you're a mean narrator.*
*You're my favourite social commentator.*
*You're my Shelley, Keats and Clare.*
*You've had more hits than Baudelaire.*

But I say nothing for the entire journey
and on arrival at Manchester Piccadilly we both leave the train
and I rush ahead to find a doorway to smoke in.
A stick-thin figure joins me there.
A man I would know anywhere,
and in slanting rain and wind that whips
we struggle with Rizlas and filter tips

and when he lights up John turns to say…
he turns to say,
'Fooking smoking ban, eh?'
and I say, 'Yeah, right?'

If I said a lengthy chat ensued then that would be a fiction,
but we shared the camaraderie of nicotine addiction,
and only when we'd gone our separate ways
I realised what I really wanted to say, and it was just
*thank you.*
Thank you kindly, Cooper Clarke, poet, raconteur and clown.
Rhythmic ranter, king of banter, metaphor and noun.
Thank you kindly, Cooper Clarke; for me you wear the crown.
You walked us down to Beasley Street and you showed us
Chickentown.

# CONGA LINE

One evening my husband said, 'Let's do a conga.
It would be short at first, but it could get longer.
We could fuel up first with a couple of rums
and I'll strike up a beat on my tumbadora drum.
We'll knock on some windows and ring a few bells
and coerce the neighbours with whistles and yells.
If you like the idea and you think that you might,
we could conga our way into Saturday night.
There may be detractors. I'm sure we'll get some,
but what if we start it and people do come?
I'll be the leader but not autocratic.
Someone must ensure our procession's not static.
And I will determine the direction of travel,
without which most congas begin to unravel.
The powers that be might express some disquiet
but concede that a conga is hardly a riot.
We'll snake past the wine bars and boarded-up shops,
luxury apartments and mean tower blocks.
Past industrial landscapes and manicured parks
as the cold light of morning replaces the dark.
We might lose our resolve as the weather gets worse
and as quick as it gathered our throng might disperse.
But can you can envisage what might come to pass
if our bountiful conga reached critical mass?
We'd be no respecters of boundary or place.
A conga so vast you can see us from space.'

So I looked at him and I said,
'No, thanks. I'd rather do the Macarena.'

# ICED GEMS

It wasn't fair that my mother disapproved of iced gems
even though she fed us lard.
Which wasn't fair.
It wasn't fair I had to nag her so hard that
when she finally gave in she was annoyed.
Which wasn't fair.
It wasn't fair that as I opened the packet it burst
and they all landed on the grimy pavement.
Which wasn't fair.
It wasn't fair to have to see all that iced biscuit loveliness
lying there and it wasn't fair that some were almost untouched
and my mother told me to *just* leave them.
So I screamed and shouted that it wasn't fair
and got in a horrible state.
Which wasn't fair.
And I wanted them more than anything.
Which wasn't fair.

Then my mother grabbed my face between her hands and
shouted,
'LIFE ISN'T FAIR.' And I said, 'Oh,'
because up until then she had led me to believe that it was.

Which wasn't fair.

# PUNCTUATING MY FATHER

I didn't know how to punctuate
the distance between us,
so I put my 'father' in quotation marks.
Later on I put him in brackets.
Then I put a full stop after him.
Now I wish it had been a comma
or at least a semicolon.
All I have left are question marks.

# GOVERNMENT RESPONSE TO THE NATION'S CHILDREN REGARDING CURRENT AND FUTURE ECOLOGICAL CRISES

we regret
the burning trees
the swelling seas
accidentally killing bees
the microplastic on the breeze
we regret
the toxic waste
the land debased
resources plundered
in our haste
we regret
the senseless greed
we had so much
we didn't need
it's not as if we didn't care
we tinkered with stuff here and there
then argued as we watched askance
declining every slender chance
maintaining there would be a lack
unless we dig and burn and frack
so we regret the poisoned earth
we didn't comprehend its worth
we'll muddle through and toss the dice
regretfully you'll pay the price

# ECO-CRIME IN SURREY

I'm so ashamed I just have to confide in someone.
I just wasn't myself that day.
The cleaner cancelled again, so I had
to let her go, and the dishwasher got stuck mid-
cycle. Millie rang three times about the tennis club
bake sale and Bertie came home from school with a raging
temperature. So then I had to get a sitter while I took
Celeste to ballet. My God, that sequinned
tutu took some sewing. Then the Range Rover was
having a service, so I had to drive the Mini, and to
cap it all the dog threw up on the Tibetan hand-
knotted rug in the snug. Then Toby set off
to Zurich without so much as a peck on the
cheek and I just carried on folding his
boxers, then I paired up the children's
socks. Nowadays he looks right through
me and he's been on the phone again
in his study and I can smell Coco Mademoiselle, not
mine, on his collar. The stain on the rug just wouldn't
come out. That was when I found myself in the kitchen,
in such a rage that I felt a disconnect with my whole
world, as if all the years of pent-up resentment were
crashing in on me at once. My heart was
thumping and the veins were throbbing behind my
eyes as I fell into a raging vortex of self-pity.

That's when I did it.

I took the yoghurt pots and the horrible slimy
clamshell containers and the empty peanut
butter jars waiting to be washed. I took
the milk cartons and egg boxes
and the avocado peelings and the Amazon
delivery crap and the leftover tiramisu.
I took the rotten bananas and I took
the mouldy cheese and the newspapers and the pizza
boxes and I threw the whole lot straight

in the rubbish bin. And then I put it out. Without a second
thought for the planet or what the neighbours might
say. I know there is no excuse and even
now I keep thinking *what if
someone finds out?* The guilt is
completely overwhelming, but of course I
wasn't myself that day.

You won't tell anyone else, will you?

# SAVAGE SUMMER

That summer was a prowling beast
with a fire in its belly.
Cats wailed and dogs howled and
the leaves were parched brown on the branches.
Babies grizzled in their cots,
their tiny fists clenched in outrage.
People unfurled umbrellas just for some blessed shade.
Further afield the Artic blazed and melted while
refugees in flimsy boats sank unreported.
Fishermen wept by the dry river beds and
the crops were puny and riddled with blight.
That summer the city boiled over,
leaving burnt-out cars and smashed windows.
Tempers were stretched and expletives and punches were
thrown.
Young men in looted trainers were frisked by the roadside.
Sirens pierced the steamy nights.
The news was of martial law and empty shelves.
That summer we held our loved ones tightly.
We tried to remember our blessings
and we learnt how to cherish the cold and wet.
When it came.

# MOTHER-IN-LAW'S DRAWER

a bag of old pennies
a Sunday missal
some baby shoes
a tarnished whistle

bent reading glasses
two Burma Stars
an old school tie
some Matchbox cars

buttons, brooches
old dog leads
some thimbles, a camera
hatpins, beads

binoculars, a horseshoe
a map of York
three embroidered hankies
a silver fish fork

chipped statuette from Portugal
rosary from Rome
extendable watch strap
probably chrome

stack of love letters
tied with string
a cracked alarm clock
that doesn't ring

no use weeping
stiff upper lip
one pile for keeping
one for the skip

# I DON'T KNOW, GO AND PLAY

*Real questions asked by small children.*

Where does the green go in winter?
Why doesn't water have bones?
When will it be yesterday?
When is a puddle a pond?

How far can you go under?
How far can you go up?
Why is the moon broken tonight?
Where do bubbles go when they pop?

Are two of anything the same?
Is a spider's web its home?
Why is the rain going sideways?
Why are snails so slow?

Can a tomato kill you?
How many years old is snow?
Has anyone counted all the stars?
Where did my shadow go?

What keeps the sky from falling down?
Why can't I see my own eyes?
I really, really need to know
if my apple is dead or alive.

# GLENDA

Once had a boss,
name of Glenda.
Put my ego
through the blender.
Hyper-critical and sly,
she loved to set
the bar too high.
With eyebrows raised
and curling lip
she presupposed
that I would slip
and celebrated every blip.
I didn't surrender to Glenda;
instead
I tried to comprehend her.
And eventually
I got HR to suspend her.

# REDUNDANCY NOTICE (I)

Given the new buy-in and the scalability
and leverage of the recent takeover
we are driving our capabilities to monetise our
operation. Due to this paradigm shift we've
drilled down and reassessed core competencies
and synergy within the organisation as well as
our mission criticality in the context of the
current macro and micro economic climate.
The upshot is that we have revaluated our
windows of opportunity for project deliverables
in the short to medium term and, given your level
of pushback, we've had to take a punt on
your net net contribution. We are now
empowered to make seamless economies of
scale with regard to our diminishing returns.
Further to this actionable repositioning you
have now been redesignated as an involuntary
entrepreneur. Due to the exigencies of the time
imperative this will come into immediate effect.

# REDUNDANCY NOTICE (II)

Alexa, order me a gun.
My job is gone, my life is done.
I gave the bosses all I've got
and now my job's done by a bot.
It took me years to learn my trade,
but automatons don't get paid.
Because of bloody tech like you
the only job's Deliveroo.
Alexa, order me a gun.
My job is gone, my life is done.

# DEAN AND DAWN

Dean's mother's brothers, Paul and Bertie,
lost theirs at the age of thirty,
and, knowing this to be a sign
of alopecia down the line,
Dean spent each day in fear and dread
of all the hair he might have shed.

Each week he begged Dawn to assess
degrees of follicle distress,
and this she did, though at the time
Dean's hair was lustrous, sleek and fine.
But as she stroked each golden tress
she wondered, would she love him less?

There wasn't very long to wait.
A thinning patch became a pate.
Dean's hair retreated like a tide,
from brow to vortex. Back and sides.

Although Dawn shared Dean's solemn grief
about his shrinking straggly wreath,
agreed with him it wasn't fair
that lesser men should keep their hair,
lost in a crowd his shining dome
was like a beacon when she roamed.
And if hair loss was a lover's test
Dawn swore she loved him more.
Not less.

# LION MIND

A therapist told me I have a dog mind.
That my troubles are like bones that I chase
as if I have no choice other than
to fret and worry each of them in turn.
Instead, he said, 'Cultivate a lion mind.
No matter how many bones are thrown around,
the lion will simply sit and stare,
keeping its eye on the bigger picture.
The bones are merely incidental to the lion
in the light of bigger prey.'

Next day I arrange myself in a comfortable pose.
I contemplate my problems.
I am non-judgemental and composed.
I am determined to cut them down to size.
My troubles simply glare back at me
and do not diminish in importance or impact.

I am still chasing bones.

Later on there is pizza.
I make sure I have the lion's share.

# NEIGHBOUR FROM HELL

My neighbour says that my garden has Japanese knotweed.
He says that my roses have blackfly.
He says that I encourage the bushy-tailed foxes that gambol at dawn.
He says that my convolvulus crept over his hedge and strangled his marigolds.
He says my neglected ecosystem is seeding wildly in his borders.
My neighbour is always on the lookout for overhanging branches.
My neighbour says that my ash tree has dieback.
He says that my tomato plants carry early blight.
He sent a letter to the council about my sinister garden gnomes.
He thinks that I climbed his fence and murdered his wisteria.
He says that I once planted onions on his lawn.
My neighbour thinks I am in league with aphids and killing all the bees.
My neighbour says that I grow leylandii to rob him of his dappled light.
He thinks that I take his loamy soil and turn it sour.
He says that I bring late frost and plagues of slugs and snails.
He says that I put hemlock and belladonna in his compost.
My neighbour thinks I can summon the hounds of hell to dump red-hot turds on his azaleas.
He thinks I can harness the entire forces of Gaia just to wreak revenge on his tiny patch.

My neighbour is wrong.

My garden does not have Japanese knotweed.

# HERSTORY LESSON

be as curious as Curie
be as brazen as Mae West
never let someone define you
or decide for you what's best
channel inner Cleopatra
battle like you're Joan of Arc
be as proud as Pocahontas
be as bold as Rosa Parks
honour all your unsung sisters
both the living and the dead
stories scattered unrecorded
on the path that you now tread
dance like Isadora Duncan
make like Maya Angelou
be a rebel and resister
herstory is down to you
trot your stuff like Tina Turner
flaunt your funk like Chaka Khan
be as blunt as Betty Boothroyd
keep repeating 'yes, I can'

# ON AGEING

the years have hit me like a truck
forgetting stuff and getting stuck
so many hairs I ought to pluck
(the creams they sell are mainly muck)
once thought about a nip and tuck
in case they see and mutter *yuck*
now more inclined to sit and cluck
wrinkles seem to run amuck

not sure I really give a fuck

# I NEVER THINK OF YOU

Last week I got my brown belt in Shaolin Kung Fu.
Played the Moonlight Sonata on a didgeridoo.
Modelled cashmere sweaters in Milan.
Sailed a twenty-eight-foot catamaran.
Designed an award-winning corporate logo.
Crossed the Brecon Beacons (partly on a pogo).
I got a boa constrictor for a family pet.
I had a poem go viral on the internet.
So I didn't think of you. No, I never think of you.

This week I'll drive to Tossa de Mar
with Danny Dyer in an open-topped car.
Sing a football anthem and entrance the nation.
Deliver a TED talk on self-motivation.
Discover a herbal cure for cancer.
Do a pas de deux with a principal dancer.
Help to solve the homeless crisis.
Broker Middle East peace. (Have a word with ISIS.)
So I won't think of you. No, I never think of you.

# HEART BEAT

See here. My heart is an open book.
That's my aorta.
Go on.
Take a look.
See pumping ventricles.
Hear that dull beat
like a visceral metronome.
See I am meat.

See here. My heart is an open book.
Inspect every chamber and
probe every nook.
I am fallible.
Culpable.
Frail.
Incomplete.
Until my last breath
I will pulse to this beat.

# ACKNOWLEDGEMENTS

Thank you to my fellow poets for being so inclusive and supportive. You know who you are. Thank you to my family. You know why.